BLUE CODE

How to communicate effectively with police officers.

Alexia L. Knox, B.A., M.P.A., M.A., LSSGB

Blue Code. How to communicate effectively with police officers.
Copyright © Alexia L. Knox, 2022.

All rights reserved.

Edited and cover designed by Genzen Agency P.O. Box 91255, Milwaukee, WI 53209. Where this book is distributed in the U.S., U.K., Australia, and the rest of the world, this is by Alexia L. Knox. Genzen Agency is a registered trademark of Nationalics company number A057105.

ISBN 979-8-9869294-0-8
ISBN 978-8-9869294-1-5 (eBook)

Genzen Agency
P.O. Box 91255
Milwaukee, WI 53209
www.genzenagency.com

CONTENTS

Introduction
Blue Code: A3 (Figure 1)

WHAT ARE POLICE OFFICERS?
Origins of Police Officers
Fraternal Order of Police
Law Enforcement Bill of Rights
Qualified Immunity Act

POLICE OFFICER TRAINING
Background checks
Training
Communication Strategy #1

EXISTING PROCEDURES: LEVELS OF FORCE
Levels 1 – 5
Communication Strategy #2
Use of Force: Escalation and De-escalation Tactics
Communication Strategy #3

WHAT IS AN ARREST?
Types of Warrants
Types of Persons
Communication Strategy #4

WHAT HAPPENS WHEN YOU ARE ARRESTED BY A POLICE OFFICER?
Standard Criminal Procedure
Types of Evidence
Exceptions
Providing a Statement to Law Enforcement
Blue Code: Command Flowchart (Figure 2)

Communication Strategy #5
Communication Strategy #6

WHAT ARE PROTECTIONS AND PRIVILEGES?
Miranda Rights
Freedom of Speech
Right Against Self-Incrimination
Right to Counsel
Duty to Intervene
Concurrent Jurisdiction

WHAT IS CONSIDERED A CRIME?
Types of Offenses
Communication Strategy #7

HOW ARE CITIZENS PROTECTED FROM POLICE MISCONDUCT?
Remedies of Citizens
Types of Police Discipline
Communication Strategy #8

WHAT TO SAY WHEN INTERACTING WITH A POLICE OFFICER
Nonverbal Responses
Blue Code: Root Cause Analysis (Figure 3)
Emotions
Communication Strategy #9
Situational Analysis
Communication Strategy #10
TCC: Ten Communication Commandments

Conclusion

INTRODUCTION

Police officers are called to respond to a crime or possible crimes. They should be, right? Crime is everywhere and we expect police officers to respond to a crime, investigate the crime, outsmart the criminal, subdue the perpetrator, interrogate them, make arrests without injury, and report the crime. Our dependency on law enforcement to perform these duties convinces me that we need law enforcement to keep our communities safe. However, ordinary folks are subject to the same treatment as a perpetrator or criminal. How does a police officer – an entity that enforces the law - tell the difference between you - the law-abiding citizen, and the perpetrator? How should a person interact with law enforcement whether or not a crime had been committed?

First, we must obey the law to limit unnecessary interactions with law enforcement.

Second, we must learn how to communicate with law enforcement to preserve our rights and privileges when interacting.

While there is a need to preserve the integrity of the police profession, people are terrified of interacting with police officers. Blue Code deciphers codes used by law enforcement to identify a growing problem of police violence against unarmed people. Blue Code will interpret statutes, color of law, fraternal order of police, power dynamics, and communication gaps between law enforcement and the public as the root cause of police violence. Blue Code shares verbal and nonverbal communication techniques used by law enforcement to design useful communication strategies people can use when interacting with police officers based on the DMADV methodology. Blue Code addresses a serious problem of police violence against unarmed people observed through online research, videos of police violence blasted on social media, and personal observations, which I experienced as a former wife of a police detective. I am not a lawyer. I am a survivor. The communication strategies listed in Blue Code saved my life, could save another person's life, and will preserve the integrity of the police profession.

My past interactions with police officers were not all bad, though. I had an enjoyable childhood that involved interacting with police officers on a daily basis.

During the community police era, police officers would "walk the beat," meaning- newly trained police officers would walk along the sidewalks of neighborhoods to increase police presence. Senior officers rarely "walked the beat," but they patrolled the streets in their squad cars and handed out baseball cards to neighborhood children. I was one of those children. Few neighborhood children were comfortable talking with police officers. We ran toward the squad car peeking through the windows looking for the bad guys – jumping up and down while asking for baseball cards. One early evening, a senior police officer named, Officer M. and his partner drove toward the creek where I and another child were playing. Officer M. and his partner pulled over and asked, "Hey! Y'all want some baseball cards?" We shouted, "Yes!" and raced to the blue and white squad car as Officer M. and his partner exited the car, opened all four doors, and stood outside of the squad car. As we touched around the surface of the interior, wide-eyed and curious - Officer M., friendly and big, chatted casually with his partner while observing our neighbors. His arms were big and muscular, just like the wrestlers we had seen on television the night before. Although we were the children who ran up to Officer M., there were many more children who ran in the other direction. I wasn't sure why they ran away from Officer M. but I always observed him watching their houses. When the street lights came on it was time for me and my friend to head home. We scurried along never knowing whether Officer M. ever communicated with the other children or their families after dark.

Times haven't changed much. Those who were forbidden from interacting with police officers as children are uncomfortable communicating with law enforcement as adults. Understandably, many of those family members and neighborhood children were eventually arrested by police officers, charged, and disproportionately sentenced for crimes in court based on zero-tolerance statutes.

It is no wonder the general public does not trust the criminal justice system. A recent Gallup poll found that the public's confidence in the U.S. Supreme Court and the criminal justice system are each down. Laws like truth-in-sentencing were passed through U.S. Congress and provided billions of dollars in grants to states and localities to build or expand correctional facilities through the 1994 Crime Act. The requirement for localities and states to qualify for the truth-in-sentencing grant was: "persons convicted of a crime had to serve at least 85% of their prison sentence." Although many states have repealed this law, the damage has already been done. The trust between law enforcement and generations of neighborhood families has become irreparable.

Nonetheless, we are trained to be citizens who must trust police officers to respond to crime and enforce statutory and civil laws. We default to trusting police officers because we expect them to perform their job duties.

But...

What if law enforcement officers habitually demonstrated aggressive and violent behaviors toward the public? What if law enforcement officers, an entire department, or several police departments chose to not discuss, prevent, or report the violent behaviors of other law enforcement officers? Over some time, such silence becomes the subculture within a police organization referred to as a 'blue wall.'

There isn't much difference between a 'blue wall' and a 'blue pill.'

The term, 'blue pill' is when a person has an oblivious perception of reality. Research shows that certain members of society are supportive of law enforcement and the criminal justice system despite the trend of violent videos that we see on social media, violations of others' rights and privileges, and the enforcement of biased policies. 'Blue pill' individuals might underreport crime, misreport crime, or commit crimes without a sense of accountability.

Crimes like homicide, murder, assault, and other violent crimes have long-lasting effects on society. Drug activity, crimes against children, robbery, vandalism, human trafficking, hate crimes, extreme violence, assault, and other crimes are on the rise in both rich and poor neighborhoods. Violent crimes are underreported in rural and suburban communities. Also, police departments do not fully report violent crimes in rural, suburban, and less populous neighborhoods compared to urban neighborhoods. In recent years, the FBI Quarterly Uniform Crime Report received crime data from only half of the law enforcement agencies in the country. We can conclude that crime data and neighborhood crime reports or statistics are not complete or conclusive. Therefore, we will not rely on too many statistics in this handbook.

Nonetheless, no matter which neighborhood we live in, communicating with a police officer can be emotional. Answering questions like, 'License and registration, please," or 'Where are you headed?' - while the officer maintains a grip on his or her service weapon - can be terrifying for many people because videos have shown police officers using deadly force.

Unfortunately, a growing number of unarmed people have become victims of police violence in these same situations.

We know the stories.

After hearing and watching the stories about violent police interactions, I had to question the communication between the officer and the person being arrested:

- 'Why didn't the person listen to the officer's commands?
- How much time does an average person have to translate those commands?
- Why did the officer use deadly force against an unarmed person?
- Why did the officer yell, "Stop resisting!"
- Was the person resisting arrest after being shot?'

Research suggests that a person's ability to process information is reduced by up to 80% during emotionally charged situations (Gilman, 2004). Therefore, improving communication between both police officers and people is fundamental to the design and implementation of the 'Blue Code.'

Figure 1

Blue Code: A3

Background	**Problem Statement**
The general public should understand the role of law enforcement and become familiar with various tactics to effectively communicate with law enforcement officers.	Police violence against unarmed people in the U.S. has shown a clear communication gap between law enforcement and the public.

Goal
The goal is to understand how law enforcement communicates and share verbal and nonverbal communication techniques used by law enforcement to identify communication barriers.

Root Cause Analysis
The current state of communications between law enforcement and the public reflects a military communications style, such as the use of commands and the application of defensive tactics intended to force compliance to those commands. The general public is not familiar with receiving commands nor aggressive or military-style communications and as a result, unarmed people are killed by law enforcement when interacting.

Proposed Corrective Action
Examine the history of law enforcement, the color of law, and compare the rights and privileges of both law enforcement officers and the general public to uncover a derivation of power and the root

Proposed Plan
Analyze verbal and nonverbal communication techniques typically used by police officers to eliminate communication gaps.

> cause of communication gaps between people and police officers.

WHAT ARE POLICE OFFICERS?

Law enforcement consists of federal agents, uniformed police officers, detectives, troopers, sheriffs, state highway patrol, game wardens, special jurisdiction officers (university and transportation authority), and other local law enforcement officials are entities that enforce laws, statutes, civil ordinances, local codes, and regulations for a specific jurisdiction. We will only be discussing police officers and statutory authority.

Police officers are entities of the government who swear to protect and serve under the statutes. The term *police offer* is defined as, "a peace officer responsible for preserving public order, promoting public safety, and preventing and detecting crime." Additionally, Black's Law Dictionary (4th Ed.), defines *police power* as, "… the power of the government to intervene in the use of privately owned property, as by subjecting it to eminent domain." The actions of police officers are protected under the Tenth Amendment, Fraternal Order of Police, Law Enforcement Officer Bill of Rights, and Qualified Immunity Act.

Origins of Police Officers

The first publicly funded police department was established in 1838 in Boston, Massachusetts. Some may argue that the first fraternal order of police officers was "paddy rollers," or "slave patrol," which was established in 1704 in South Carolina. Slave patrols were utilized by Virginia, New York, Massachusetts, Maryland, Rhode Island, Connecticut, New Hampshire, Delaware, North Carolina, South Carolina, New Jersey, Pennsylvania, and Georgia, before any statehood or signage of the U.S. Constitution. In 1661, the role of law enforcement was first utilized in Maryland and was called, "constables." Slave patrol or "constables" were equipped with whips, guns, and other weapons to chase, search, harass, apprehend, interrogate, detain, assault, and murder targeted groups across the Thirteen Colonies.

In 1905, local police officers became a national organization under the ideologies of August Vollmer, the founder of the police profession and creator of the Uniform Crime Report Program.

Other law enforcement establishment dates:

- 1865 – U.S. Secret Service.
- 1908 – Federal Bureau of Investigation.
- 1915 – Fraternal Order of Police.

Tenth Amendment

"The powers not delegated to the United States by the Constitution, nor prohibited by it to the states, are reserved to the States respectively, or to the people."

- Ratified on December 15, 1791

Fraternal Order of Police

The Fraternal Order of Police consists of over 355,000 police officers in the United States. It is the world's largest social organization for law enforcement officers and its allegiance is to the United States of America. The introduction of the organization states, "…We are committed to improving the working conditions of law enforcement officers and the safety of those we serve through education, legislation, information, community involvement, and employee representation." The organization also provides fellowship and other services to its members.

Law Enforcement Bill of Rights

Law Enforcement Bill of Rights or LEOBR legislation was passed in several states. Law enforcement rights are written in most states' statutes. Under LEOBR, law enforcement officers are protected from investigations and prosecution when acting within their official capacity.

Depending on the state, LEOBRs allow law enforcement departments to investigate misconduct allegations of other law enforcement officers between different departments and there is no civilian oversight. Usually, a panel of fellow police officers governs the actions and behavior of police officers.

LEOBR:

- Except when on duty or acting in an official capacity, have the right to engage in political activity or run for elective office.

- Shall, if disciplinary action is expected, be notified of the investigation, the nature of the alleged violation, and be notified of the outcome of the investigation, and the recommendations made to superiors by the investigators.

- Questioning of a law enforcement officer should be conducted for a reasonable length of time and preferably while the officer is on duty unless exigent circumstances apply.

- Questioning of the law enforcement officer should take place at the offices of those conducting the investigation or at the place where the officer reports to work unless the officer consents to another location.

- Will be questioned by a single investigator, and he or she shall be informed of the name, rank, and command of the officer conducting the investigation.

- Those under investigation are entitled to have counsel or any other individual of their choice present at the interrogation.

- Cannot be threatened, harassed, or promised rewards to induce the answering of any question.

- Are entitled to a hearing, with notification in advance of the date, access to transcripts, and other relevant documents and evidence generated by the hearing, and representation by counsel or another non-attorney representative at the hearing.

- Shall have the opportunity to comment in writing on any adverse materials placed in his or her personnel file.

- Cannot be subject to retaliation for the exercise of these or any other rights under Federal, or State.

Qualified Immunity Act

The American Bar Association defines Qualified Immunity (Act) as: "A judicial doctrine created by the Supreme Court that shields state actors from liability for their misconduct, even when they break the law. Under this doctrine, government agents—including but not limited to police officers—can never be sued for violating someone's civil rights, unless they violated 'established law.'"

In 1967, the Qualified Immunity Act was justified through a U.S. Supreme Court case based on the fact that a police officer, who is a state actor under the color of law, has probable cause for an arrest and a good faith belief of an offense, should not be punished for its legal authority.

POLICE OFFICER TRAINING

The organizational structure of law enforcement is similar to a military chain of command. Police officers and military personnel must follow a line of authority and duty. Police officers are accustomed to performing duties consisting of controlling the behaviors of others and promoting order under statutory law. People are expected to participate or agree with orders provided by a police officer. Although many police officers display emotional triggers, qualified police officers are trained on how to give orders through the use of interpersonal communication techniques to effectively perform their duties. Also, the use of both private and public funds, federal and state grants, taxes, budgets, local fees, fines, forfeitures, and special assessments are used to fund background checks and progressive police training.

Background checks

Before police officers are hired, they undergo several background checks. They must meet educational requirements and pass several criminal background checks, financial background checks, and psychological background checks. Many police departments do not use psychological background checks.

Training

Police Officers receive more than 1,000 hours of advanced training.

Police officers are certified and qualified to perform their jobs. They complete and pass continuous field training consisting of law, mediation, negotiations, crisis intervention, self-defense, physical combat, and firearms. Additional training is provided related to investigating homicides, deaths, injuries, child injuries, forensics, ballistics, and other areas.

After training and demonstrating advanced knowledge of collecting evidence, police officers become P.O.S.T. certified ("Peace Operation Specialized Training") and are referred to as, peace officers and are allowed to act as law enforcement officials during employment, while off-duty, and throughout retirement.

COMMUNICATION STRATEGY #1

Maintain eye contact.

EXISTING PROCEDURES: LEVELS OF FORCE

Police officers can use various levels of force when performing their jobs. There are existing procedures or escalation and de-escalation tactics used during the application of five levels of force:

Level 1 - Their Presence
Level 2 - Verbal Commands
Level 3 - Empty Hand Control
Level 4 - Less Lethal Methods
Level 5 - Lethal Force

Level 1 - Presence

Police officer presence serves as a visible representation of law and order.

Examples:

- Marked vehicle
- Squad car
- Sirens
- Red and Blue Lights
- Uniformed officer
- Badge

Level 2 - Verbal Commands

Verbal commands are the audible representation of law and order providing lawful commands to a person.

Verbal commands include words, oral control, and paralanguage, such as the use of tone and voice inflection.

An officer's ability to communicate with others is their most valuable tool.

Examples:

- Hello. What seems to be the problem?
- Glad you're enjoying the day. Do you know how fast you were going?
- Is everything okay? Do you have any medical issues I should know about?
- Do you have a weapon that I should know about?
- May I have your license and registration?
- Stop! Or I will shoot!
- Don't move!
- Put your hands up!
- Put your hands on your head!
- Put your hands on the steering wheel!
- Put your hands where I can see them!
- Let me see your hands!
- Face down on the ground!
- Get out of the car!
- Gun!

Level 3 - Empty Hand Control

Nonverbal commands are used as body language deception tactics, which include intimidation and manipulation.

Examples:

- Placing hands on service weapon
- Tuck hands in vest
- Facial expressions
- Gestures
- Proxemics
- Eye contact
- Standing with legs apart
- Holding flashlight overhand

Level 4 - Less Lethal Methods

Officers may use pain compliance methods, such as physical force and defensive tactics to apprehend a suspect and force compliance to commands. Law enforcement can cause bodily harm when other levels of force cannot be used.

Examples:

- Tear gas
- Taser gun
- Baton strikes
- Inflict pain for compliance
- Open hand strikes to vulnerable areas
- Pulling hair
- Twisting arms
- Body strikes

- Foot traps
- Wrist locks/grabs/twists
- Head butt
- Knee strikes
- Knee on belly
- Knee on neck without rendering unconsciousness (banned in some states)
- Pressure on pressure points
- Boxing
- Pinching
- Hold restraints
- Chokeholds (banned in some states)
- Chokehold from behind
- Body locks (banned in some states)
- Surprise attacks

Level 5 - Lethal Force

Officers may use lethal force when extremely necessary in combination with verbal commands, such as a verbal warning before a shot with their service weapon. Lethal force is used when other levels of force cannot be used under certain circumstances:

Examples:

- Deadly force through the use of serious bodily harm.
- Deadly force through the use of a service weapon.

Law enforcement officers can use deadly force in the following situations:

- Self-defense
- Preventing a crime similar in nature that might cause death or bodily harm to another person.
- During an apprehending of a person believed to have committed a similar crime that presents an imminent danger of death or serious bodily harm.
- Preventing the escape of a person believed to have committed a similar crime that presents an imminent danger of death or serious bodily harm.
- Preventing an escape by use of a weapon or explosive.

COMMUNICATION STRATEGY #2

Show your hands when communicating.

Escalation and De-escalation Tactics as a Use of Force:

- Verbal commands are used to control your actions and intimidate you.

- Nonverbals and body language are used to give commands and de-escalate a situation.

- Force can be used to enforce compliance.

- Lethal force can be applied in most circumstances.

- Switching between forces is routine.

- Manipulation tactics are used to collect evidence, draft incident reports, and testify in court.

- Oral control is an escalation tactic.

- Body cameras can be turned on and off.

- Hearsay can be used as evidence in certain circumstances.

- Distraction and the element of surprise can be applied when using force.

- Sucker punch or the use of combat-style force before, during, and after a lawful command is an escalation and de-escalation tactic.

- Friendly interactions are used to collect evidence, such as through the use of one or more body cameras.

- The use of sight, sense of smell, and hearing can be used as probable cause to search your person, vehicle, home, or personal property for evidence of a crime.

COMMUNICATION STRATEGY #3

Observe escalation and de-escalation tactics.

WHAT IS AN ARREST?

Police officers are progressively trained to enforce the law by arresting different types of persons with a warrant or a warrant from a judge. Typically, police officers make arrests of *persons,* and arrests of private citizens or noncitizens can occur when a crime has been committed. When making a warrantless arrest, police officers should have:

- Jurisdiction
- Reasonable belief that the arrest is necessary.
- Personal observation of the crime.
- Probable cause that a person(s) committed or will commit a crime.

Types of Warrants

- Arrest Warrant
- Search Warrant
- Child Support Warrant
- No-Knock Warrant
- Bench Warrant
- Other types of warrants are defined in statutes or local laws.

The term 'arrest' means the legal authority to deprive a person of his or her freedom of movement. I found out that the term 'arrest' is not defined in any constitutional law, Code of Criminal Procedure, or other acts, but is defined and described in statutes, which means the term can have various definitions depending on the state or locality.

When a person is arrested for committing a violent or nonviolent offense against city, county, or state statutory or civil laws, their 'person' and the freedom of movement conferred to it is subject to that jurisdiction where the offense was committed.

Statutes

Statutes are bills or acts enacted by a legislative body such as a state, city, or county. These bills and acts become rules or laws of that state, city, or county organized as institutions or entities.

Citizens adhere to statutes. Becoming a citizen subjects your 'person' to statutory law.

Types of Persons
(Based on Merriam-Webster Dictionary since 1828)

Person of Interest
A person who is believed to be possibly involved in a crime but has not been charged or arrested.

Suspect
A person suspected of a crime.

Detainee

A person held in custody, especially for political reasons.

Subject
A person who has engaged in activity that a federal prosecutor has identified as being within the scope of a federal grand jury investigation.

Target
A person against whom a federal prosecutor has substantial evidence of involvement in criminal activity and whom the prosecutor believes is likely to be indicted by a grand jury.

COMMUNICATION STRATEGY #4

Use your knowledge of the law.

WHAT HAPPENS WHEN YOU ARE ARRESTED BY A POLICE OFFICER?

First, you should know that when a person is accused of a criminal offense, federal or state prosecutors use the evidence collected from local police officers when deciding to use a grand jury to indict a person.

An indictment is defined as, *"the formal written accusation of a crime, made by a grand jury and presented to a court for prosecution against the accused person."*

Law enforcement must follow rules outlined in the criminal procedure when arresting someone. Generally, the following stages are based on those rules, which are standard.

Standard Criminal Procedure

The arresting officer must have PROBABLE CAUSE
to execute a SEARCH & SEIZURE
to collect EVIDENCE
to validate an ARREST
and charge a person with a CRIMINAL OFFENSE.

Search & Seizure

Law enforcement must have permission to search or seize you or your property. They must also collect evidence to justify a search, seizure, or arrest. When evidence is collected under a lawful search and seizure, an arrest can be made and a criminal offense can be assessed to the person suspected of committing a crime described under the statutes against the state and/or jurisdiction.

NOTE: If you consent to a search, any evidence collected, as described under the law, can justify an arrest.

Investigations

Law enforcement officers are required to investigate alleged crimes based on probable cause and the collection of evidence that would support an arrest or other lawful acts of law enforcement. Unfortunately, some evidence is not as clear and an officer's probable cause to act within the law is an ongoing story to tell.

Here is an example of being charged with an offense:

While performing a traffic watch, a police officer observed a driver speeding through a red light. The police officer used sirens and lights to pull over the driver. The officer exited the squad car, placed a fingerprint on the passenger side tail light, approached the vehicle, and confronted the driver. While walking toward the vehicle, the officer observed a shiny object with a black rubber handle on the back seat of the vehicle. The driver was visibly shaken and appeared to have scratches below her left eye. The officer made a verbal command to the driver to provide her license and registration. The driver provided her license and registration. The officer proceeded to initiate an interrogation, "Do you know how fast you were going? Did you notice that you went through a red light?" The driver began to quickly move her hands in the air while aggressively shouting at the officer. The police officer commanded the driver to get out of the car as bystanders observed the interaction nearby. The driver became hysterical, yelled at the police officer, and did not exit the car or comply with the officer's command. The police officer opened the car door and pulled the driver out of the car window by her hair yelling, "Get on the ground! Stop resisting!" The police officer tasered the driver on the lower extremity, numbing her legs to force compliance. She was placed in handcuffs and thrown in the back seat of the squad car. The officer initiated a search of her vehicle due to there being a reasonable belief that a crime would have taken place after observing a traffic offense, facial injury, and obstructive behavior. The police officer believed there was probable cause to search the vehicle. After searching the vehicle, there were no weapons found. Upon returning to the vehicle, the driver was observed hitting her head against the squad car window. The officer opened the door to subdue the driver to prevent any further harm to herself or others. The person spat on the police officer. The police officer grabbed the suspect and was headbutted. The police officer used his firearm and discharged his service weapon killing the unarmed woman. The person was charged with obstruction of justice before dying from her injuries but was never arrested.

This scenario also shows that there could have been clearer communication between the officer and the person.

COMMUNICATION STRATEGY #5

Demonstrate civil behavior and remain calm.

Types of Evidence

When interacting with police officers, evidence is tricky and there are so many rules to consider. There are several types of evidence that police officers use to justify a search, seizure, or arrest.

According to the Black's Law Dictionary (1996),

Evidence n. (14c) - 1. Something that tends to prove or disprove the existence of an alleged fact. 2. The collective mass of things esp. testimony and exhibits, are presented before a tribunal in a given dispute. 3. The body of law regulating the admissibility of what is offered as proof in the record of a legal proceeding. – evidence, vb.

Below are common types of evidence used by the criminal justice system and collected via law enforcement:

- *Probable Cause.* (16c) A reasonable ground to suspect that a person has committed or is committing a crime or that a place contains specific items connected with a crime.

- *Circumstantial Evidence.* (18c) 1. Evidence-based on interference and not on personal knowledge or observation. 2. All evidence that is not given by eyewitness testimony.

- *Clear and Convincing Evidence.* (17c) Evidence indicating that the thing to be proved is highly probable or reasonably certain.

- *Corroborating Evidence.* (17c) Evidence that comes from different sources and is often irreconcilable.

- *Direct Evidence.* (16c) Evidence that is based on personal knowledge or observation and that, if true, proves a fact without interference or presumption.

- *Illegally Obtained Evidence.* (1924) Evidence obtained by violating a statute or a person's constitutional or another right, especially the Fourth Amendment guarantee against unreasonable searches, the Fifth Amendment right to remain silent, or the Sixth Amendment right to counsel.

- *Opinion Evidence.* (18c) A witness's belief, thought, interference, or conclusion concerning a fact or facts.

- *Original Evidence.* (18c) A witness's statement that he or she perceived a fact in issue by one of the five senses., or that the witness was in a particular physical or mental state.

- *Partial Evidence.* (17c) Evidence that establishes one of a series of facts.

- *Prima Facie Evidence.* (18c) Evidence that will establish a fact or sustain a judgment unless contradictory evidence is produced.

- *Real Evidence.* (17c) Physical evidence (such as clothing or a knife wound) that itself plays a direct part in the incident in question.

- *Substantive Evidence.* The evidence offered to help establish a fact in issue, as opposed to evidence directed to impeach or to support a witness's credibility.

- *Tangible Evidence.* Physical evidence that is either real or demonstrative.

- *Testimonial Evidence.* (1831) A person's testimony offered to prove the truth of the matter asserted; especially, evidence elicited from a witness.

- *Documentary Evidence*: documents including digital records of communications, and so on, produced as evidence to the court.

COMMUNICATION STRATEGY #6

Create distance between yourself and the officer.

Exceptions

When evidence is collected during an unlawful search and seizure, that evidence is excluded, unless a statement of good faith is provided by a law enforcement officer, which can be used in court as evidence.

A good faith exception must show that a police officer had a reasonable, good-faith belief that they (the officer) acted according to legal authority. As a result of their good faith belief, the illegally seized evidence can then be admissible and used as evidence. Also, when evidence is unlawfully seized to justify an arrest, a police officer can provide a statement or affidavit regarding the character of a person during the arrest. This affidavit might demonstrate that a reasonable person would have seized evidence lawfully or unlawfully to make credible their actions. Good faith statements and affidavits provided by a police officer are sworn statements and can be considered evidence.

There are exceptions to using hearsay under certain circumstances.

Providing a Statement to Law Enforcement

Before and during an arrest, a police officer may ask for a statement. The purpose of the statement is to investigate a crime and collect evidence. Statements are admissible in court and usually cannot be changed. It is very common to forget important details and be falsely accused of a crime or falsely accuse someone else.

A police officer may obtain actual or fabricated evidence, such as a statement from a witness during, before, or after an arrest to justify an arrest.

Below is a flowchart that outlines the process of communication between police officers and a suspect/person. Communication is limited to commands and the suspect or person understanding and complying with those commands. When a person does not comply with those commands police officers can use force.

Figure 2

Blue Code: Command Flowchart

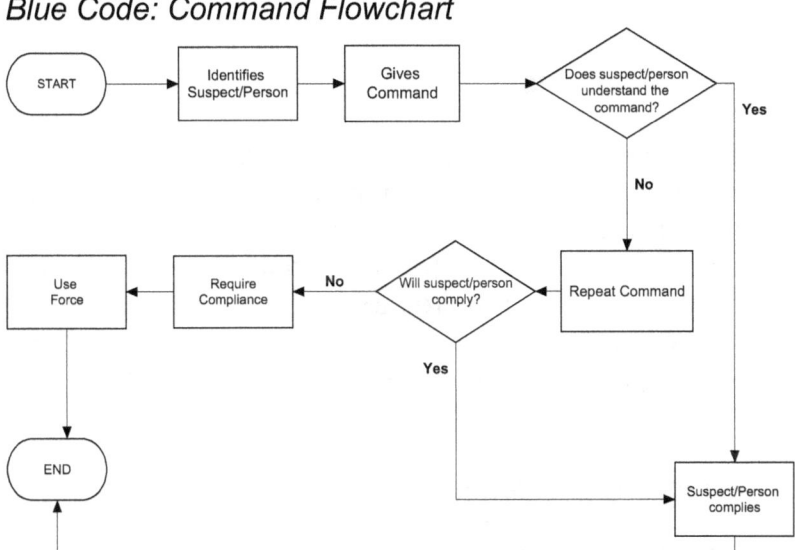

WHAT ARE PROTECTIONS AND PRIVILEGES?

There are federal laws that protect all persons in the United States and address police misconduct. Also, in the U.S., there are "protections and privileges" afforded to people who are subject to local, statutory law, or civil law.

Miranda Rights or Miranda Warning, Freedom of Speech, Right Against Self-Incrimination, Right to Counsel, Confront Witnesses, and Speedy Trial, and Duty to Intervene are just a few examples of "protections and privileges."

Miranda Rights

The term "Miranda Rights" is based on the Fifth and Sixth Amendments. Miranda Rights protect against a person providing self-incriminating statements to law enforcement and a person's right to an attorney. Officers are not required to read out Miranda Rights unless a person is in police custody and being interrogated about a crime.

Miranda Rights reads,

"You have the right to remain silent. Anything you say can and will be used against you in a court of law. You have the right to an attorney. If you cannot afford an attorney, one will be provided for you. Do you understand the rights I have just read to you? With these rights in mind, do you wish to speak to me?

Freedom of Speech

The Supreme Court ruled that people can say almost whatever they want to each other and law enforcement officers. "The Court said that it's important that people be free to choose their words... Even if those words are angry, even words that are seen as offensive words." Also, inflammatory speech is protected by the Constitution but the Court made a distinction between speech that promotes crime, speech that incites immediate crime, and using obscenities in a public place against a specific person, which is unlawful and violates the First Amendment.

The First Amendment text reads:

"Congress shall make no law respecting an establishing of religion, or prohibiting the free exercise thereof, or abridging the freedom of speech, or the press, or the right of the people peaceably to assemble, and to petition the Government for a redress of grievances."

Right Against Self-Incrimination

The Fifth Amendment text reads:

"No person shall be held to answer for a capital, or otherwise, infamous crime, unless on a presentment or indictment of a Grand Jury, except in cases arising in the land or naval forces, or in the Militia, when in actual service in time of war or public danger; nor shall any person be subject for the same offense to be twice put in jeopardy of life or limb; nor shall be compelled in any criminal case to be a witness against himself, nor be deprived of life, liberty, or property, without due process of law; nor shall private property be taken for public use, without just compensation."

Right to Counsel, Confront Witnesses, and Speedy Trial

The Sixth Amendment text reads:

"In all criminal prosecutions, the accused shall enjoy the right to a speedy and public trial, by an impartial jury of the State and district wherein the crime shall have been committed, which district shall have been previously ascertained by law, and to be informed of the nature and cause of the accusation; to be confronted with the witnesses against him; to have compulsory process for obtaining witnesses in his favor, and to have the Assistance of Counsel for his defense."

Duty to Intervene Law

The Duty to Intervene Law is a federal cause of action against state officials who deprive private citizens of their constitutional rights.

Section 1983 of the Civil Rights Act of 1871 reads:

"Every person who under color of any statute, ordinance, regulation custom or usage of any State or Territory or the District of Columbia, subjects, or causes to be subjected, any citizen of the United States or other person within the jurisdiction thereof to the deprivation of any rights, privileges or immunities secured by the Constitution and laws, shall be liable to the party injured in an action at law, suit in equity, or other proper proceeding for redress…"

Further, the United States Court of Appeals described the standard for being liable for failure to intervene as:

"... an officer who is present and fails to intervene to prevent other law enforcement officers from infringing the constitutional rights of citizens is liable under § 1983 if that officer had reason to know: (1) that excessive force was being used, (2) that a citizen has been unjustifiably arrested, or (3) that any constitutional violation has been committed by a law enforcement official; and the officer had a realistic opportunity to intervene to prevent the harm from occurring."

Concurrent Jurisdiction

When crimes are committed within a state or local jurisdiction, federal law can also be applied concurrently. For example, a police officer committed an offense similar to a hate crime against a citizen in Georgia during an arrest. The State of Georgia charged the police officer with a crime and the federal government charged the police officer with a federal offense, such as a hate crime.

According to Black's Law Dictionary, concurrent jurisdiction means,

"[t]he jurisdiction of several different tribunals, each authorized to deal with the same subject matter at the choice of the suitor." Black's Law Dictionary, 363 (Revised 4th ed. 1968).

WHAT IS CONSIDERED A CRIME?

A crime is considered an offense against public law. A person can commit a crime against both federal and state laws but we will only discuss criminal offenses against state laws as described by the U.S. Department of Justice (DOJ) and Federal Bureau of Investigation (FBI). The federal government categorizes offenses against public law as 'crimes.' State and local law enforcement agencies report some of their crime data to the federal government.

The following offenses or crimes were substantiated with arrests made by state and local law enforcement and are reported to the FBI through the Uniform Crime Report Program.

NOTE: The Federal Bureau of Investigation (FBI) investigates cybercrime, public corruption, hate crimes, human trafficking, white-collar crime, and violent crime.

This list does not contain all statutory crimes:

Types of Offenses

Criminal Homicide - Murder and nonnegligent manslaughter: the willful (nonnegligent) killing of one human being by another. Deaths caused by negligence attempts to kill, assaults to kill, suicides, and accidental deaths are excluded. The program classifies justifiable homicides separately and limits the definition to: (1) the killing of a felon by a law enforcement officer in the line of duty; or (2) the killing of a felon, during the commission of a felony, by a private citizen. b.) Manslaughter by negligence: the killing of another person through gross negligence. Deaths of persons due to their negligence, accidental deaths not resulting from gross negligence, and traffic fatalities are not included in the category Manslaughter by Negligence.

Forcible rape - Rapes by force and attempts or assaults to rape, regardless of the age of the victim, are included in federal statutes. Statutory offenses (no force used—victim under the age of consent) are excluded.

Robbery - The taking or attempting to take anything of value from the care, custody, or control of a person or persons by force or threat of force or violence and/or by putting the victim in fear.

Aggravated assault - An unlawful attack by one person upon another to inflict severe or aggravated bodily injury. This type of assault usually is accompanied by the use of a weapon or by means likely to produce death or great bodily harm. Simple assaults are excluded.

Burglary (breaking or entering) - The unlawful entry of a structure to commit a felony or theft. Attempted forcible entry is included.

Larceny-theft (except motor vehicle theft) - The unlawful taking, carrying, leading, or riding away of property from the possession or constructive possession of another. Examples are thefts of bicycles, motor vehicle parts, and accessories, shoplifting, pocket-picking, or the stealing of any property or article that is not taken by force and violence or by fraud. Attempted larcenies are included. Embezzlement, confidence games, forgery, check fraud, etc., are excluded.

Motor vehicle theft - The theft or attempted theft of a motor vehicle. A motor vehicle is self-propelled and runs on land surfaces and not on rails. Motorboats, construction equipment, airplanes, and farming equipment are specifically excluded from this category.

Arson - Any willful or malicious burning or attempt to burn, with or without intent to defraud, a dwelling house, public building, motor vehicle or aircraft, personal property of another, etc.

Other assaults (simple) - Assaults and attempted assaults where no weapon was used or no serious or aggravated injury resulted to the victim. Stalking, intimidation, coercion, and hazing are included.

Forgery and counterfeiting - The altering, copying, or imitating of something, without authority or right, with the intent to deceive or defraud bypassing the copy or thing altered or imitated as that which is original or genuine; or the selling, buying, or possession of an altered, copied or imitated thing with the intent to deceive or defraud. Attempts are included.

Fraud - The intentional perversion of the truth to induce another person or other entity in reliance upon it to part with something of value or to surrender a legal right. Fraudulent conversion and obtaining of money or property by false pretenses. Confidence games and bad checks, except forgeries and counterfeiting, are included.

Embezzlement - The unlawful misappropriation or misapplication by an offender to his/her use or purpose of money, property, or some other thing of value entrusted to his/her care, custody, or control.

Stolen property - Buying, receiving, possessing, selling, concealing, or transporting any property with the knowledge that it has been unlawfully taken, as by burglary, embezzlement, fraud, larceny, robbery, etc. Attempts are included.

Vandalism - To willfully or maliciously destroy, injure, disfigure, or deface any public or private property, real or personal, without the consent of the owner or person having custody or control by cutting, tearing, breaking, marking, painting, drawing, covering with filth, or any other such means as may be specified by local law. Attempts are included.

Weapons (carrying, possessing, etc.) - The violation of laws or ordinances prohibiting the manufacture, sale, purchase, transportation, possession, concealment, or use of firearms, cutting instruments, explosives, and incendiary devices, or other deadly weapons. Attempts are included.

Prostitution and commercialized vice - The unlawful promotion of or participation in sexual activities for profit, including attempts. To solicit customers or transport persons for prostitution purposes; to own, manage, or operate a dwelling or other establishment to provide a place where prostitution is performed; or to otherwise assist or promote prostitution.

Sex offenses (except forcible rape, prostitution, and commercialized vice) - Offenses against chastity, common decency, morals, and the like. Incest, indecent exposure, and statutory rape are included. Attempts are included.

Drug abuse violations - The violation of laws prohibiting the production, distribution, and/or use of certain controlled substances. The unlawful cultivation, manufacture, distribution, sale, purchase, use, possession, transportation, or importation of any controlled drug or narcotic substance. Arrests for violations of state and local laws, specifically those relating to the unlawful possession, sale, use, growing, manufacturing, and making of narcotic drugs.

Gambling - To unlawfully bet or wager money or something else of value; assist, promote, or operate a game of chance for money or some other stake; possess or transmit wagering information; manufacture, sell, purchase, possess, or transport gambling equipment, devices, or goods; or tamper with the outcome of a sporting event or contest to gain a gambling advantage.

Offenses against the family and children - Unlawful nonviolent acts by a family member (or legal guardian) that threaten the physical, mental, or economic well-being or morals of another family member and that are not classifiable as other offenses, such as Assault or Sex Offenses. Attempts are included.

Driving under the influence - Driving or operating a motor vehicle or common carrier while mentally or physically impaired as the result of consuming an alcoholic beverage or using a drug or narcotic.

Liquor laws - The violation of state or local laws or ordinances prohibiting the manufacture, sale, purchase, transportation, possession, or use of alcoholic beverages, not including driving under the influence and drunkenness. Federal violations are excluded.

Drunkenness - To drink alcoholic beverages to the extent that one's mental faculties and physical coordination are substantially impaired. Driving under the influence is excluded.

Disorderly conduct - Any behavior that tends to disturb public peace or decorum, scandalize the community, or shock the public sense of morality.

Vagrancy - The violation of a court order, regulation, ordinance, or law requiring the withdrawal of persons from the streets or other specified areas; prohibiting persons from remaining in an area or place in an idle or aimless manner; or prohibiting persons from going from place to place without visible means of support.

Suspicion - Arrested for no specific offense and released without formal charges being placed.

Curfew and loitering laws (persons under age 18) - Violations by juveniles of local curfew or loitering ordinances.

All other offenses - All violations described under state or local laws are not specifically identified in this list.

COMMUNICATION STRATEGY #7

Cooperate. Understand a police officer's sensitivity to victims.

HOW ARE CITIZENS PROTECTED FROM POLICE MISCONDUCT?

Citizens are provided privileges outlined in the Civil Rights Act of 1964, Fourth Amendment, Fifth Amendment, Fourteenth Amendment, Color of law 18 USC 241, 242, and other legislation. Citizens who report law enforcement misconduct do have certain remedies when a police officer acts outside of his/her official capacity and violate a person's freedom, rights, or privileges under the U.S. Constitution, Bill of Rights, International Bill of Human Rights, Civil Rights, or religious rights. Also, law enforcement officers do not have special protections outlined in the U.S. Constitution.

Remedies of Citizens

The Fourth Amendment states,

"The right of the people to be secure in their persons, houses, papers, and effects, against unreasonable searches and seizures, shall not be violated, and no warrants shall issue, but upon probable cause, supported by oath or affirmation, and particularly describing the place to be searched, and the persons or things to be seized."

Citizens and non-citizens can utilize the following processes:

- Contact the law enforcement agency involved.

- Ask for a supervisor.

- File a formal complaint against police officers.

- Send a written complaint to the officer's supervisor or chief of the police department.

- Report police misconduct to the internal affairs division of the police department.

- Submit a written complaint to the U.S. Department of Justice.

- Contact a lawyer, violence prevention organization, media, or social media to draw attention.

COMMUNICATION STRATEGY #8

Be careful what you say or choose to be silent.

Types of Police Discipline

- Complaint listed on personnel record
- Suspension
- Demotion
- Administrative Leave (Paid/Unpaid)
- Forced retirement
- Termination
- Civil lawsuit
- Criminal charges
- Probation
- Prison

Under LEOBR, police officers can keep their jobs and maintain their salary during informal investigations which are conducted by a panel of fellow police officers.

WHAT TO SAY WHEN INTERACTING WITH A POLICE OFFICER

Any reasonable person accused of a crime would want to explain their innocence or deny their guilt to a police officer when they have been identified as a suspect. The process of communicating with a police officer is complex particularly because there are emotions involved, paralanguage, commands, and a power imbalance that might cause communication issues.

Communication techniques such as tone, proxemics, facial expressions, paralanguage, oculesics (eye movement, blink rate, etc.), and emotion can be applied or interpreted as a threat to safety. There are clever verbal and nonverbal communication methods a police officer might use when interacting with people:

Nonverbal responses:

- Eye contact
- Calm demeanor
- Limit facial expression
- Place both hands on the waist or top of the head (in view)
- Listen closely
- Use a louder than your normal tone of voice
- Blink faster than normal
- Apply several feet of distance
- Upright posture
- Appropriate dress

Emotions

Law enforcement officers display the following emotions such as anger, fear, frustration, bias, and others. I recall watching a video about a police officer attacking an innocent bystander. The hostility demonstrated by that officer was disturbing. Another video showed an officer forcefully grabbing the neck of a female officer who tried to prevent that officer from harassing a suspect who was handcuffed.

The current state of communications between law enforcement and the public reflects a military communications style. The use of commands, yelling those commands, and the application of defensive tactics intended to force compliance to those commands are used in the military and are defined as aggressive communications. The general public is not familiar with receiving commands nor aggressive or military-style communications. As a result, unarmed people are killed by law enforcement when communicating with law enforcement.

In the next section I will use 'Five Whys,' a root cause analysis tool, to help uncover the underlying origin of a problem described earlier:

Problem:

"Police violence against unarmed people in the U.S. has shown a clear communication gap between law enforcement and the public."

Figure 3

Blue Code: Five Whys Root Cause Analysis

Why won't the public listen to the commands of police officers?

Because the general public does not understand military-style commands.

Why isn't the general public familiar with military-style commands?

Because the characteristics of military-style communications are aggressive which is socially unacceptable.

Why are aggressive communications used by law enforcement considering their unacceptability?

Because police officers are trained to use aggressive communication to resolve conflict and manage crime-related emergencies. An aggressive communication style may be used as a level of force during interactions with the public.

Why are police officers trained to use an aggressive communication style even when there is no conflict (i.e., a traffic stop)?

Because police officers are permitted to use any level of force to enforce a command and justify their use.

Why hasn't the general public been educated about the various levels of force used by police officers, including the use of aggressive communication-style commands?

Because police organizations have not identified or acknowledged that there is a gap between how a person and a police officer communicate.

Research has shown that on-duty officers may not communicate well with other officers. The root cause of police violence against unarmed people can be attributed to a lack of communication training for law enforcement or a communication gap between law enforcement and the public. An additional communication barrier is underlying emotions. Anger, blame, fear, frustration, hate, and other emotions might attribute to law enforcement officers not communicating effectively.

Examples:

Anger

Police officers have become angry at people who do not comply with their commands. Police officers are taunted, insulted, ridiculed, or harassed by citizens, victims, suspects, entire communities, or colleagues and have become angry when they feel disrespected. I have seen law enforcement display anger when they believe they believe someone is or has been dishonest. Also, law enforcement has family problems, experience divorce, stress on the job, substance abuse, peer pressure, and low self-esteem that could cause anger and be displayed on the job.

Blame

Police officers patrol our communities daily. They respond to emergencies involving victims of crime and create reports of those crimes. Over time, police officers may create blame theories to rationalize why crimes are being committed. They may attribute one or more causes to another person's behavior to achieve control of their environment. Many police officers are promoted to detectives because they have learned to use blame to demonstrate cognitive control of their environment.

Fear

Police officers expect to interact with non-compliant and disorderly citizens who break the law or might attempt to break the law. Police officers can fear for their safety and the safety of others when interacting with disorderly individuals or groups. Unfamiliar settings, uncertainty, or dissimilar people may cause fear when performing their jobs.

Frustration

Interviewing victims of violence or solving victimless crimes can be frustrating. Police officers may need to collect information from witnesses, suspects, and victims all while sorting through numerous statements to make an arrest, determine a motive, or something else within short time frames. Interacting with people can cause frustration when a person does not comply with verbal commands or escalations and de-escalations. Also, I have seen law enforcement become frustrated with a victim when the victim decided not to pursue criminal charges after having collected evidence.

Hate

A police officer can demonstrate hate when there is rage, disgust, resentment, neglect, hostility, violence, prejudice, or discrimination towards specific individuals belonging to a certain race, gender, social class, religion, sexual orientation, disability, or other members of society.

Bias

Police officers can be biased toward members of a specific group. Biased-based policing can be demonstrated without conscious awareness. Research has shown that implicit and explicit biases in policing are attributed to communication barriers between police officers and the community it serves.

Out of Order

When law enforcement officers are 'out of order' their behavior is unacceptable, defective, and unlawful. An officer who acts 'out of order' is acting unlawfully and outside the scope of their assigned duties. Police brutality, excessive force, unnecessary high-speed chases, and corruption are behavioral examples of an officer being out of order. When an officer is out of order their interactions are usually observed by the public who are determined to record and monitor these behaviors for their safety and the safety of others.

Trust

Police officers are entrusted to perform their jobs and they rely on other officers for their safety. Typically, the public does not trust police officers and so they choose to not interact with them. When an officer is not trusted by the community it serves, the presence of law enforcement may feel like a terror to a community rather than protection from crime. Many police officers demonstrate complacency, low morale, develop a superiority complex, and biases when communicating with a community that chooses to not interact with them.

Strength Contest

Whether or not a person can physically overpower a police officer, outshoot them, or outrun them should be irrelevant but some people choose to interact with police officers by testing an officer's physical ability to arrest them. Law enforcement officers have used commands and have escalated levels of force to subdue a person. I saw a video of a police officer tackling a man to the ground, sitting on his back, and the suspect refused to give the officer his hands. The officer discharged his weapon and shot the suspect in the back of the head. Law enforcement has applied unnecessary and excessive force when interacting with people and suspects. Unfortunately, many people have been killed by law enforcement.

COMMUNICATION STRATEGY #9

Observe the officer's emotions and hands.

Situational Analysis

Now that we have nine communication strategies to refer to, let's test them out by using the following hypothetical situations:

Situation: Traffic Stop
Communication Strategy #1: Maintain eye contact

Whenever an officer pulls you over during a traffic stop you need to have your license and registration prepared before interacting. When interacting with a police officer, always maintain direct eye contact. Eye contact shows that you are serious and prepared for the interaction.

Situation: Possession of a Firearm
Communication Strategy #2: Show your hands when communicating.

Carrying a weapon, possessing a weapon, or having a weapon in plain sight is a right for many. If approached by a police officer it might be best to show your hands, tell the officer that you have a weapon in your possession, and where that weapon is located. Ask for instructions regarding what to do with your weapon while showing your hands. This open communication might protect you from a potentially deadly situation.

Situation: Suspicion and Sudden Movements
Communication Strategy #3: Observe escalation and de-escalation tactics.

When an officer approaches you with their hands on their service weapon, they are warning you that they are escalating their levels of force. When an officer places their hands in their vests they are de-escalating their levels of force. People may feel emotional when encountering police officers. When a police officer uses an aggressive communication style it may cause a person to become nervous, fearful, or confused. A person may make sudden movements or gestures that might require a police officer to make a split-second decision to escalate their use of force to protect their safety and the safety of others.

Situation: Knowing Your Rights
Communication Strategy #4: Use your knowledge of the law.

Police officers might assume that you do not know your rights or the law. Familiarize yourself with legalese and statutes. When communicating with a police officer, do not be shy about your knowledge of the law. Demonstrate your knowledge. This is important because using their language reminds the officer that they can be accountable if acting outside of their authority.

Situation: Searches, Seizures, and Arrest
Communication Strategy #5: Demonstrate civil behavior and remain calm.

An officer can request permission to search you, your property, and your vehicle to establish probable cause. Calmly tell the officer, "I do not consent to a search." Or ask, "Why are you searching my property? I did not consent to a search. Please do not search my personal property." (Wouldn't you like to know why an officer would ask to search your yard, house, pockets, purse, etc.?) Also, if you are being placed in handcuffs, ask the police officer, "Am I being arrested? "Why am I being arrested?" or "Why am I being detained?" Police officers can seize your device during interrogation if they have a warrant, if the person using the phone was involved in illegal activities, or if the phone contains evidence.

Situation: Reasonable Suspicion
Communication Strategy #6: Create distance between yourself and the officer.

Situations can be dangerous when an officer is suspicious of you or when they believe their lives are endangered. Police officers can use necessary force to protect themselves and others if they believe that you are a threat.

There are many videos online showing police officers responding aggressively to citizens who record them on their cell phones. When recording or interacting with a police officer, it is best to stand clear from physical contact with officers and to create distance to be within the view of a body camera just in case the police officer escalates their level of force.

Situation: Victimhood
Communications Strategy #7: Cooperate. Understand a police officer's sensitivity to victims.

When a person is harmed or killed by someone, the victim(s) and their families rely on law enforcement to make an arrest. Police officers are committed to solving crimes and conflicts on behalf of crime victims. It is important to understand a police officer's sensitivity to victims and their commitment to upholding the law. Cooperate with police officers because it makes their jobs easier and our neighborhoods safer.

Situation: Interrogation
Communications Strategy #8: Be careful what you say or choose to be silent.

When a person is accused of a crime or identified as a suspect it is their right to remain silent while being interrogated. It may not be effective for a person to be silent when a police officer gives a command. I believe that a person should communicate: "Officer, I UNDER-stand," while complying with the command to survive the emotionally-charged interaction.

Situation: Cellphone
Communication Strategy #9: Observe the officer's emotions and hands.

There is a recording device available via our cellphones or an officer's body camera. When an officer makes an arrest or performs an interrogation to justify an arrest it is important to know that you have a right to be silent. Watch the officer's hands and movements to observe escalations and the functionality of the body camera. In recent years, there has been discussion about the constitutionality of communication companies sharing mobile phone data with law enforcement during an investigation. Concerns about privacy rights have been raised regarding the Stored Communications Act.

Situation: Horseplay

Communication Strategy #10: Observe body language and use both verbal and nonverbal responses.

> Many police officers are highly trained for serious crimes and responding to minor activities can be considered a waste of their valuable skills. Playful behaviors and a lack of respect toward police officers may cause an officer to become irritated. Irritation can translate to body language, eye contact, verbal, and nonverbal responses to people. So, if you catch yourself being a bit too wild or playful around police officers, calm down or leave their presence.

In addition to the situations listed above, here are a few more caveats.

Be aware that a police officer can:

- Combine lies and facts to collect evidence and make an arrest.

- Use media and press conferences to release unsubstantiated information to make an arrest.

- Separate witnesses when collecting evidence.

- Confiscate your cell phones without a warrant.

- Place a person in handcuffs and not arrest them.

- Can strip-search a person in public and not arrest them.

- Use silence against you when you are being accused.

- Use your rights, such as, the right to bear arms, as reasonable suspicion to investigate crime.

- Use reasonable force to arrest you.

- Use drones and K-9s (police-trained canines) to perform a lawful search.

- Use the data from cell phone towers and cell-site simulators to obtain a warrant.

- Use video from private and public security cameras as reasonable suspicion.

- Use public video from street or pole cameras to execute a warrant.

- Use reasonable suspicion to detain and not arrest you.

COMMUNICATION STRATEGY #10

Observe body language and use both verbal and nonverbal responses.

TCC: Ten Communication Commandments for Police Officers:

1. Be empathetic.
2. Remain calm.
3. Maintain eye contact.
4. Show your hands when communicating.
5. Identity yourself by name, badge number, and position.
6. State your reason for the interaction.
7. Immediately disclose whether the person is a witness, person of interest, suspect, target, or being interrogated.
8. Provide auditory warning when escalating levels of force.
9. Know when not to use deadly force.
10. Do not abuse your power.

CONCLUSION

In this handbook, we addressed how people can communicate with law enforcement and have posited how law enforcement should communicate with the public. Community-oriented policing sets a reasonable expectation or benchmark for how law enforcement can interact and communicate with people.

When police officers walk or drive the beat, they build rapport with people to effectively solve crime. Law enforcement does not have to be a militarized civil force in communities that utilizes escalated and high levels of force and an aggressive communication style consisting of commands. These tactics have only widened the communication gap between law enforcement and the public. Police officers have a responsibility to the public to communicate with them as human beings to close this communication gap.

Now more than ever police organizations must act to avoid becoming a terror among the public. Community relations must be improved to preserve the integrity of law enforcement as a profession and to protect victims of crime. Legislation related to embedding social workers in police departments, recording and reporting police misconduct, decertifying officers, and promoting duty to intervene laws is a strong position towards reducing biased-based policing. Promoting de-escalation tactics within police organizations, implementing tier-level employment systems that permit the use of levels of force, enhanced background screenings of police officers, and promoting a cultural lens to policing should be advanced in developing and achieving collaborative police reform goals.

I can write about these ideas in future research papers.

Law enforcement organizations in the United States of America have the opportunity to demonstrate something other than bias, emotion, and violence in their policing practices. Police departments across the United States of America have an opportunity and the authority to implement change and employ the smartest and most efficient approach to policing.

The world is watching.

REFERENCES

911MEDIA. (2021, November 17). *About the fraternal order of police*. Fraternal Order of Police. Retrieved February 22, 2022, from https://fop.net/about-the-fop/

Addressing police misconduct laws enforced by the Department of Justice. The United States Department of Justice. (2020, October 13). Retrieved February 22, 2022, from https://www.justice.gov/crt/addressing-police-misconduct-laws-enforced-department-justice

Americanbar.org. (n.d.). Retrieved February 22, 2022, from https://www.americanbar.org/groups/public_education/publications/insights-on-law-and-society/volume-21/issue-1/qualified-immunity/

Apex officer - virtual reality police training simulator. Apex Officer - Virtual Reality Police Training Simulator. (n.d.). Retrieved February 22, 2022, from https://www.apexofficer.com/

Author Unknown. (n.d.). *Distinction/difference between arrest and custody*. SRD Law Notes. Retrieved February 22, 2022, from https://www.srdlawnotes.com/2019/01/distinctiondifference-between-arrest.html

Black's Law Dictionary - *Free Online Legal Dictionary*. The Law Dictionary. (2022, February 7). Retrieved March 29, 2022, from https://thelawdictionary.org/

Brenan, M. (2021, November 20). *Americans' confidence in major U.S. institutions dips*. Gallup.com. Retrieved February 22, 2022, from https://news.gallup.com/poll/352316/americans-confidence-major-institutions-dips.aspx

Gilman, R., Meyers, J., & Perez, L. (2003, December 9). *Structured extracurricular activities among adolescents: Findings and implications for school psychologists.* Wiley Online Library. Retrieved February 22, 2022, from https://onlinelibrary.wiley.com/doi/abs/10.1002/pits.10136

Global Study on Homicide - United Nations Office on drugs ... (n.d.). Retrieved February 22, 2022, from https://www.unodc.org/documents/data-and-analysis/gsh/Booklet1.pdf

Global Study on Homicide. United Nations: Office on Drugs and Crime. (n.d.). Retrieved February 22, 2022, from https://www.unodc.org/unodc/en/data-and-analysis/global-study-on-homicide.html

Horton, J. (2021, May 17). *How US police training compares with the rest of the world.* BBC News. Retrieved February 22, 2022, from https://www.bbc.com/news/world-us-canada-56834733

Knox, A. L. (n.d.). *Police reform: Understanding interspersed social influences and the propagation of public policy during covid19.* STARS. Retrieved February 22, 2022, from https://doi.org/10.30658/icrcc.2021.17

Stopped by police. Know Your Rights | American Civil Liberties Union. (n.d.). Retrieved February 22, 2022, from https://www.aclu.org/know-your-rights/stopped-by-police/#ive-been-stopped-by-the-police-in-public

www.ingramcontent.com/pod-product-compliance
Lightning Source LLC
Chambersburg PA
CBHW070857050426
42453CB00012B/2245